NATURE'S LIGHT SHOW

COMETS

By Kristen Rajczak

Gareth Stevens
Publishing

Please visit our website, www.garethstevens.com. For a free color catalog of all our high-quality books, call toll free 1-800-542-2595 or fax 1-877-542-2596.

Library of Congress Cataloging-in-Publication Data

Rajczak, Kristen.
Comets / Kristen Rajczak.
    p. cm. — (Nature's light show)
Includes index.
ISBN 978-1-4339-7020-7 (pbk.)
ISBN 978-1-4339-7021-4 (6-pack)
ISBN 978-1-4339-7019-1 (library binding)
1. Comets—Juvenile literature. I. Title.
QB721.5.R35 2013
523.6—dc23

                                        2011045163

First Edition

Published in 2013 by
Gareth Stevens Publishing
111 East 14th Street, Suite 349
New York, NY 10003

Copyright © 2013 Gareth Stevens Publishing

Designer: Katelyn E. Reynolds
Editor: Kristen Rajczak

Photo credits: Cover, p. 1, (cover, pp. 1, 3–24 background) Digital Vision/Thinkstock; (cover, pp. 1, 3–24 graphics), pp. 6, 10, 11, 18, 20, 21 Shutterstock.com; p. 4 European Space Agency/NASA; p. 5 European Southern Observatory/NASA; p. 7 (image) NASA/JPL–Caltech/UMD; p. 7 (illustration) NASA/Steele Hill; p. 8 Lunar and Planetary Institute/NASA; p. 9 Kauko Helavuo/Stone/Getty Images; p. 13 NASA; p. 15 Stocktrek/Brand X Pictures/Getty Images; p. 16 Dorling Kindersley/Getty Images; p. 17 Lodriguss Jerry/Photo Researchers/Getty Images; p. 19 David Nunuk/Science Photo Library/Getty Images.

Printed in the United States of America

CPSIA compliance information: Batch #CS12GS: For further information contact Gareth Stevens, New York, New York at 1-800-542-2595.

CONTENTS

Words in the glossary appear in **bold** type the first time they are used in the text.

LIGHTING UP THE SKY

In June 2010, **astronomers** said to look up! A very bright comet called McNaught C/2009 R1 was passing close to Earth and could be seen by the naked eye. Its long tail shone green in the sky, a fuzzy smear of light best seen before sunrise.

Comets are heavenly bodies, as are planets, moons, and stars. They travel millions of miles before we see them as they move closer to the sun. And some put on quite a light show!

Comet NEAT/2002 V1 streaks across the sky in January 2003.

Comets formed from the same gas, dust, and matter that became the planets. The leftover planetary material came together in the outer reaches of space and froze into large chunks.

Many comets, including the one pictured here, are named after Australian astronomer Robert H. McNaught. This one is sometimes called the Great Comet of 2007 because of its bright tail.

COMET HISTORY

Comets have been observed and recorded by humans for thousands of years. From about the 4th century BC, comets were believed to come from Earth. It wasn't until the 16th century that comets were proved to be **celestial** objects.

In the late 1600s, scientist Isaac Newton used math to show that comets **orbited** in space. His friend Edmond Halley used this idea to find out more about 24 comets that had been reported many times. He found that comets have an **elliptical** orbit.

Edmond Halley
(1656–1742)

EYE ON THE SKY

Some ancient people believed the arrival of a comet meant that a flood, sickness, or the death of a king would soon follow.

This image shows comet 103P/Hartley 2 surrounded by a gas cloud and an illustration of its elliptical orbit in space.

Comet 103P/Hartley 2

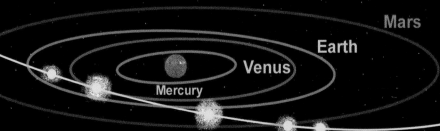

Mars

Earth

Venus

Mercury

9/14/2010

9/30/2010

11/04/2010

11/30/2010

12/12/2010

7

WHAT IS A COMET?

Comets have three parts: nucleus, coma, and tail. The nucleus is made of ice, dust, and other matter. It's the heart of the comet and the only part that always exists.

When a comet approaches the sun, the coma forms as dust, gas, and **water vapor** are pulled off by the sun's heat and energy. It looks like a fuzzy cloud around the nucleus. A comet's tail also forms as it nears the sun. Comets may have a dust tail or an **ion** tail.

dust tail

ion tail

dust trail

sun

Comets leave behind a trail of dust and other small matter as they move through space.

tail

nucleus

coma

Since ancient times, comet tails have been described as looking hairy. The word "comet" comes from a Greek word that means "hairy one."

A comet's nucleus can be many miles across. Its tail can be millions of miles long!

ASTEROID, METEOROID, OR COMET?

Comets are similar to other space objects. Asteroids are big pieces of rock orbiting in the solar system. They come from an asteroid belt between Mars and Jupiter. Meteoroids are smaller than asteroids and are made of rock and other matter from space. When a meteoroid enters Earth's **atmosphere**, it's called a meteor.

However, a comet's orbit is less regular than an asteroid's. Its nucleus contains **chemicals** in addition to the rock and space matter of asteroids and meteoroids.

When a meteor falls to Earth, it's called a meteorite. This one was found in Arizona.

A large meteorite created Barringer Crater in Arizona about 49,000 years ago. However, most meteorites that fall to Earth are very small.

EYE ON THE SKY

Asteroids can also be called minor planets.

THE KUIPER BELT AND OORT CLOUD

Comets can be found in two different areas of our solar system. They're called the Kuiper belt and the Oort cloud.

The Kuiper belt exists beyond Neptune's orbit, about 30 to 100 astronomical units (AU) away from the sun. It's shaped like a disc and contains hundreds of millions of comets and other small celestial bodies.

The Oort cloud is even farther away! Astronomers believe it's 50,000 AU from the sun and surrounds the solar system like a bubble.

An astronomical unit is equal to the distance from Earth to the sun, almost 93 million miles (150 million km).

Kuiper belt

The orange ring shows the typical orbit of an object from the Kuiper belt. The other colored rings show the orbits of planets in our solar system.

Oort cloud

The Oort cloud could contain as many as a trillion comets or small celestial bodies!

COMET MOVEMENT

Comets leave both the Kuiper belt and the Oort cloud because they're affected by the **gravity** of a nearby planet or star. These bodies give the comet a "push" toward the sun.

Comets are grouped by the length of their orbit as well as where they come from. Comets from the Kuiper belt are called short-period comets. They commonly have an orbit that lasts less than 200 years. Oort cloud comets are called long-period comets. These comets have orbits that can take thousands of years.

EYE ON THE SKY

When a comet reaches the point of its orbit farthest from the sun, it's at "aphelion." When it's closest to the sun, the comet is at "perihelion."

HALLEY'S COMET

Halley's comet is one of the most famous comets astronomers are studying today. In 1705, Edmond Halley showed that comets observed in 1531, 1607, and 1682 were the same comet, passing by Earth about every 76 years. When the comet returned during the year he **predicted** it would, it was named after him.

The last time Halley's comet passed Earth was during 1985 and 1986. During this orbit, it was photographed up close by spacecraft. Halley's comet should pass Earth again in 2061.

This illustration shows the path of Halley's comet through our solar system in light blue.

Chinese astronomers were the first to spot Halley's comet around the year 240 BC.

Halley's comet was bright enough for many people to see as it passed Earth in 1985 and 1986.

17

OTHER FAMOUS COMETS

Comet Hale-Bopp was first spotted in the sky in 1995. It had a bright coma and a long, white dust tail that was easily seen even though it didn't come very close to Earth.

Comet Holmes was first observed in 1892. Until 2007, however, it was hard to see without a **telescope**. In October 2007, comet Holmes amazed astronomers by becoming a million times brighter and appearing larger than the sun! It had burst and shot pieces of itself into space.

This photograph of comet Holmes shows how large and bright it looked compared with the stars around it.

Here, comet Hale-Bopp is shown from the top of Mauna Loa, a volcano in Hawaii.

EYE ON THE SKY

Comets are most often seen around sunrise and sunset.

SPOTTING COMETS

Today, only the brightest and largest comets can be seen without a telescope. Streetlights and other lights make it hard to see celestial bodies. That's why you can see more stars when you go camping or visit the country.

However, you can still spot comets! Astronomers often let the public know when large comets are passing close to Earth. If you see a comet at another time, you can report it. The first person to report a new comet has it named after them!

In 1996, this comet was spotted in Japan by Yuji Hyakutake. It's called comet Hyakutake!

IS THAT A COMET?

If you've heard a comet will be passing by Earth, grab your telescope and look up! But how do you know what you're seeing is a comet?

Look for shooting stars. These streaks of light, or meteors, often "fall" from a comet's tail as it moves past Earth.

Look for a cloudy, glowing spot in the sky. This is the comet's tail, which can be seen because of sun shining on its gases and dust.

Comets move in set paths and are often observable for days or months at a time. So if you miss a comet one night, try again the next!

GLOSSARY

astronomer: a person who studies the movements and makeup of the stars, planets, and other heavenly bodies

atmosphere: the gases surrounding Earth

celestial: having to do with the sky

chemical: matter that causes a change when mixed with other matter

elliptical: in the shape of an ellipse, or an oval

gravity: the force that pulls celestial bodies toward each other

ion: a small bit of matter that has an electrical charge

orbit: to move in a set path around the sun. Also, the movement around the sun.

predict: to guess what will happen in the future based on facts

telescope: a scientific instrument that allows objects far away, especially in space, to be seen

water vapor: water in the form of a gas

FOR MORE INFORMATION

Books

Carson, Mary Kay. *Far-Out Guide to Asteroids and Comets*. Berkeley Heights, NJ: Bailey Books, 2011.

Farrell, John. *Stargazer's Alphabet: Night-Sky Wonders from A to Z*. Honesdale, PA: Boyds Mills Press, 2007.

Kortenkamp, Steve. *Asteroids, Comets, and Meteroids*. Mankato, MN: Capstone Press, 2012.

Websites

ESA Kids: Comets and Meteors
www.esa.int/esaKIDSen/Cometsandmeteors.html
Learn more about comets and meteors on the European Space Agency's website for kids.

NASA Kids' Club
www.nasa.gov/audience/forkids/kidsclub/flash/index.html
Play games, watch videos, and read more about space and exploring our solar system.

Solar System: Comets
ethemes.missouri.edu/themes/255
Use these helpful and fun links to find out more about comets.

INDEX